The Problem with Abundance

The Problem with Abundance
prose poems
Charles Rafferty

GRAYSON BOOKS
West Hartford, CT
graysonbooks.com

The Problem with Abundance
Copyright © 2019, Charles Rafferty
published by Grayson Books
West Hartford, Connecticut

ISBN: 978-1-7335567-5-0

Book & Cover Design: Cindy Stewart

Acknowledgments

AMP — Airport Finches

Apeiron Review — The Empire of Silence

Arsenic Lobster — The Satin Lining of the Casket Reminds Me of a Jewelry Box

Barrow Street — A River of Birds, Preference

Beloit Poetry Journal — Moon, Poetry

Descant — Evidence

Diaphanous — The Problem With Abundance

Plume — Cold, Uncle Brian, On Hearing That Another Friend Is Dying

Prime Number Magazine — After Heavy Rain

South 85 — Parts Along Every River

82 — Inventory, The Quickness of Miracles Unbelieved

Superstition Review — Ars Poetica

The Cincinnati Review — Greetings

The New Yorker — Pond

The Southern Review — The Roman Names, Inadvertent Mousetrap, Marbles

For Scott Wolfman

Contents

Greetings	13
The Pond	14
A River of Birds	15
Marbles	16
The Roman Names	17
Airport Finches	18
Parts Along Every River	19
Uncle Brian	20
The Satin Lining of the Casket Reminds Me of a Jewelry Box	21
The Problem with Putting "Audubon" in the Name of the Local Nature Center	22
Question	23
Evidence	24
Moon	25
The Problem with Abundance	26
Anthropocene	27
The Most Beautiful Piece of Chocolate Cake You've Ever Seen	28
The American Wars	29
Things I've Seen Written in Golden Letters	30
Inadvertent Mousetrap	31
Cold	32
Preference	33
The Empire of Silence	34
On Hearing That Another Friend Is Dying	35
The Quickness of Miracles Unbelieved	36
Inventory	37
After Heavy Rain	38
Poetry	39
Ars Poetica	40
Coda	42
About the Author	43

Greetings

I counted the water towers, I counted the active smokestacks. These were the breadcrumbs I thought would lead me back. Now I know it's possible to drive so far we forget why we left, that the journey continues even after the car breaks down. I used to think I had no message, but the message is me—bloodshot and hungry, spilled coffee down the front of my shirt. People of the future, gather round. I have traveled through ink to greet you.

The Pond

The world is in short supply. This field of goldenrod will never be enough, and the ocean feels suddenly crossable. In every apple an orchard waits, but who has 20 years to cultivate it? Above our house, the contrails of the jets have turned into actual clouds. The rain they promise is another lie. Meanwhile, the taste of my blood implies that I am rusting, that a broken machine lies half-submerged in the pond I carry with me.

A River of Birds

A river of birds filled the sky above his house. It went on for days. That many animals can't be wrong, he reasoned, as he waited for the frost to blossom. He thought about his prospects: a half tank of gas, the cabinets full of soup. Later, when the river went dry, he endured its blue and empty channel. The birds that remained were different. They shook once against the cold. They sat on the wires and looked down on him, undeterred by the lack of bounty.

Marbles

At a certain point "manic depression" became "bipolar disorder." The world has always been in flux. Just look at the sky. There are fewer stars now than when I was a boy. I cannot say who took them, I cannot remember the pictures that they made. Consider Istanbul. It used to be Constantinople, and before that Byzantium. Nothing endures. I had a jaw men wanted to punch. Now the ground I stand upon feels like it's made of marbles. In Wyoming, they've just begun hunting the grizzly bear again. It is finally safe enough to be killed. I can't get over it. My teeth were once a dazzling white, all three of my brothers were living.

The Roman Names

Zeus became Jupiter and so forth. That was the first diminishment. Then Christianity seeped in and cracked the boulder of Rome. When you lose territory to the god of meekness, it's hard to keep your swagger. The temples fell into disrepair. The ash on the altars washed away. True, the planets still bear the Roman names, but how many of us notice them as we're taking our taxi down the esplanade? How many of us are certain that they are not merely stars?

Airport Finches

The finches inside the Frontier terminal have attained a kind of afterlife. While snow builds up on the tarmac, they enjoy a guilty warmth. Here they have learned to live without darkness. They have forgotten the taste of worms. Sometimes, as they flit from chair back to plastic plant, they think about the door that let them in—like a tear in the bag that shatters your wine and shows how the street is thirsty.

Parts Along Every River

Mist filled up the valley like a clogged sink. He could no longer see the tops of the river trees, and he took it on faith that the water kept going, sluggish and full of hidden fish. Back at home, his wife was waiting for an answer, and he kept turning it over like a bone he'd found, trying to guess the animal. He knew there were parts along every river where you cannot tell which way the water is moving—even if you're standing next to it, even if you immerse yourself in the wetness that has come that far.

Uncle Brian

Forty years ago, he gave me a piece of coral from the Philippines, where he'd met his first wife. She left him shortly thereafter, but I still have the coral. Bone white, the shape of an ear—it fits inside my fist. I doubt he remembered giving it to me, and because he died last Tuesday, I picked it from the little dish of keepsakes on our coffee table. Even the first wife made it to the funeral, but I stayed home and thought about coral—an animal whose skeleton is suited for display.

The Satin Lining of the Casket Reminds Me of a Jewelry Box

Consider the brooches of the dead, the wedding rings, the lockets full of faces. Assuming they don't get stolen by the men with shovels, such ornaments outlast everything. They are a kind of death tax, a toll on the way to oblivion. It isn't just jewelry. There are Bibles and flowers and lucky stuffed animals. We pack them in like we're burying pharaohs, like there's a pyramid of grief above them. And there is—but it's smaller, and made of sand, in a land that won't stop raining.

The Problem With Putting "Audubon" in the Name of the Local Nature Center

Before he could paint the birds, he had to murder them. Everyone forgets that part.

Question

What kind of gun legislation would we have if 26 senators died crouching in their offices while the sunlight was dazzling the pens upon their desks?

Evidence

On the map I have, the topographic lines of this hill look like God forgot to wipe away his fingerprint before he got in his Bible and fled. I knew one of the murdered boys. I had handed him a tissue once, to wipe his nose, as my daughter played piano at her recital. The apologists are full of mysterious ways, but I know evil when I see it. I can feel the thumb above me now, pressing down, fitting the grooves of this hillside.

Moon

The dirty monocle stares down at us. It is keeping the birds awake. Somewhere, the tides are rising, drowning the shoreline stone by stone. It is worse than coffee. I cannot read by this light; I cannot discern the colors of my map. Only worry can thrive beneath this strange eye, and no matter how hard I hurl these rocks, it will not look away.

The Problem with Abundance

The Library of Congress started out with 740 books. Now there are 838 miles of filled shelves. At one time we could have contained what the library contained. Now we are awash in what we can never read. Sitting here on my bench, among the pigeons and the indigent, I feel like a monkey about to enter a freighter breaking apart on the American sandbar. It is packed to the ceiling with bananas and plums—the weatherman calling for flies.

Anthropocene

Here at the end of it, the President is on TV, making good on all his promises. We'll be known as a thin layer of plastic and radioactive concrete squeezed between other rocks. But I'm an optimist. It could happen again—the wayward mutations proceeding to the same lucky point. The sun will last to 10 billion years; it's only been here 5.

The Most Beautiful Piece of Chocolate Cake That You've Ever Seen

We don't speak about the future anymore. We indulge the present tense: *There's an eyelash in my eggs. The dog is scratching to be let out.* At the lake, we don't listen as it talks about the sky. We're done with that. We take our steak deep-fried. We resume our cigarettes. The idea of them killing us, suddenly quaint.

The American Wars

We turn them off with a button. Meanwhile, at the local mall, soldiers wearing camouflage blend in with the pretty girls and clearance racks. Every day the list gets longer. We keep our music loud enough so no one tries to talk.

Things I've Seen Written in Golden Letters

My name in the snowbank, for one, after a long night of beer and multivitamins. Bible covers. The calling cards of car salesmen. Mostly it's things that want to seem rarefied but that are actually quite common—high school diplomas, the signage on Trump buildings.

Inadvertent Mousetrap

The moon doesn't look different despite our having been there. That's the exception. Even the slopes of Everest are stained with urine and the bodies of fallen climbers. Just look at Brooklyn. It used to be farms, and before that, forests. Last November, I stood a bottle in the shed. By the time the lilacs had broken out, the bottle was full of dead mice. It's just another story, another attempt at tranquility, undone by our lightest touch.

Cold

The berries on the cedar tree turn purple and the waxwings descend. They know a feast when they see one. As for me, the early darkness disorients until the stars come on where they have always been. My neighbor's boat is back behind his house again, wrapped in plastic. Sometimes he forgets to turn his floodlights off, deterring prowlers but ruining the sky. At bedtime, we listen to the field mice finding the old ways back inside. My wife curls into me. Tomorrow, she says, I'll need to put out the traps.

Preference

Sometimes I'll hear a sound in the swamp, and I can't tell if it's coming from an insect or a frog or a bird. But town sounds are impossible to misinterpret. Here, the car is rattling again. Here, my shoulder clicks when I reach for the oatmeal. These sounds mean money and diminishment. The repair shop I use is always cold, and the pot is full of yesterday's coffee. I pour a cup anyway and listen to the whir of spinning tools taking my car apart piece by piece. I know what's coming. I prefer the mystery of little bells drifting above dark water.

The Empire of Silence

The smoke of the snuffed candle is twice silent. It cannot be seen as it moves among the cellos in the house of the blind musician.

On Hearing That Another Friend Is Dying

I don't believe every snowflake is different. How many have we even checked? Over the centuries of microscopy, perhaps we've examined a single wheelbarrow full of snow. People are so much more complex, and yet there are twins everywhere. You're meeting them all the time and don't realize it, because they don't act like they're living in a Doublemint commercial. On a day like this, the sameness of the world is staggering. Someone drops money and the wrong person picks it up. The bees refuse to share their flowers.

The Quickness of Miracles Unbelieved

I look up and the clouds are sneaking away again. They are no better than foxes. Despite the thorns, the berries all go missing. It makes me think that, if I had one brief illness that kept me to my bed, I might miss the forsythia's tantrum between our yard and the neighbor's. Face it, the meteors are happening as we sleep, and the hummingbird won't wait until you can grab a camera. Too slow, too slow—whatever got into our neighbor's trash is already back inside its hole.

Inventory

When the wind is right, I can hear the prison's PA system drifting out of the woods. There's a mouse nest inside the bluebird box. There's a broken chainsaw inside the shed. It's not all bad. We have three guitars, a full set of china without any chips, a leaking pipe that has somehow self-repaired. I love this family. The parakeets have their way with the financial section, and the mortgage continues without hope of commutation.

After Heavy Rain

You can no longer see the kicked-over leaves where the deer ascended this hillside. The river mud has flattened out, and the gutters have lost their voice. True, there is no obvious route away from where you stand. But the hermit thrush masters its song merely by hatching, and the landslide always ends at the bottom of your ravine.

Poetry

Suffering is the only footprint that refuses to wash away, if only because we keep freshening the path, pushing our toes into the water-flattened sand as we head for the gunmetal sea.

Ars Poetica

1. I used to think of the prose poem as a mule—a sterile hybrid. Now, I see it as a euglena—that cutthroat survivor with a foot in two kingdoms.

2. Every good poem has form. To say otherwise is like saying some water doesn't have temperature.

3. To have successful poems over the long haul, you must be the kind of person who dusts the furniture when there is no hope of visitors.

4. Write every day. No one can shoot a nickel off the back of a galloping ox with just one bullet. The most one bullet will get you is a dead ox.

5. Beware of autobiography. The thing that is most accessible is not always the best material for a poem. There's a reason the pyramids were not constructed of sand.

6. Some poems fail because of just one word—as troubling as a hornet on the railing of a crib.

7. The impulse that begins a poem is almost never strong enough to finish it. The poet must let go of what ceases to be useful—like laying down your walking stick when the crags turn into plains.

8. A first book is like gristle coughed onto the dining room table. Getting it out allows you to keep breathing, but nobody wants to pick it up.

9. Poets in America are fourth magnitude stars floating above Manhattan, with everyone's night vision ruined by Instagram and football.

Coda

You believe you hear the clicking of the cello player's case and wonder why the lights have not returned. It's only me tripping on a cord as I come back to the mic. Before you leave, I want to make sure we understand each other. I did it for love and I did it for pettiness. I'll forgive you if you can't tell which. Now it's up to you to clear a thin spot on a shelf where people pass.

About the Author

Charles Rafferty's most recent collections of poems are *The Smoke of Horses* (BOA Editions, 2017) and *Something an Atheist Might Bring Up at a Cocktail Party* (Mayapple Press, 2018). His poems have appeared in *The New Yorker, O, Oprah Magazine, Prairie Schooner,* and *Ploughshares.* His stories have appeared in *The Southern Review* and *New World Writing,* and his story collection is *Saturday Night at Magellan's* (Fomite Press, 2013). He has won grants from the National Endowment for the Arts and the Connecticut Commission on Culture and Tourism, as well as the 2016 NANO Fiction Prize. Currently, Rafferty directs the MFA program at Albertus Magnus College and teaches at the Westport Writers' Workshop.

www.ingramcontent.com/pod-product-compliance
Lightning Source LLC
Chambersburg PA
CBHW021639080526
44584CB00015BA/1593